Early Years & Key Stage 1 Teachers

Literacy & Numeracy

ICT Skills for Teachers

Making effective use of Word & PowerPoint

by
Georgina Stein and Heidi Barton

Published by

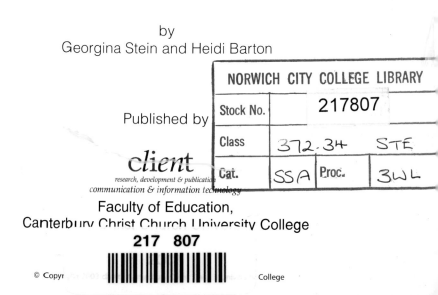

client

research, development & publication
communication & information technology

Faculty of Education,
Canterbury Christ Church University College

217 807

© Copyr... College

client

research, development & publication
communication & information technology

Published by client [c&it]
Faculty of Education
Canterbury Christ Church University College
North Holmes Road
Canterbury
Kent CT1 1QU
Tel: 01227 782802
Fax: 01227 785828
E-mail: client@cant.ac.uk
Website: http://client.cant.ac.uk

© Georgina Stein and Heidi Barton

Contributors:
Jennifer Wilkinson, Nyree Scott and
Laura Smith

First Published 2003

ISBN 1 899 253 661

Great Ideas for Early Years and Key Stage 1 Teachers has been designed to increase teachers' competence and confidence in the use of Information and Communications Technology (ICT) in the classroom and a variety of Early Years and Key Stage 1 settings.

Other titles published by client:

'How to…' flip-guides series:

- MS Word & PowerPoint
- MS Excel & Access
- MS FrontPage & Publisher
- Primary Software: Starting Graph, Number Magic, Decisions[3], Information Magic, SuperLogo and Roamer World.
- SMART Board

Technologies Inc.

Further information
SMART Interactive Whiteboards
email: smartinfo@steljes.co.uk
tel: 08000 151603

Printed on environmentally friendly paper from sustainable resources by parkers of Canterbury 766555

Contents

Great ICT Ideas
for Early Years & Key Stage 1 Teachers
Using Word & PowerPoint

LITERACY

ICT & Communication, Language and Literacy
Using Word

ICT & Communication, Language and Literacy
Using PowerPoint

client ✔

Contents

Contents

ICT, Literacy & Numeracy
Making effective use of MS Word and PowerPoint in the Classroom

Great ICT Ideas for Early Years and Key Stage 1 Teachers has been designed to increase your competence and confidence in the use of Information and Communications Technology (ICT) in the Classroom.

The activities contained within this book are relevant to teachers and adults working in a variety of Early Years and Key Stage 1 settings.

If you have some basic ICT skills and you would like to find out how easy it is to create stimulating materials with and for your children, you will find the twenty MS Word and the twenty PowerPoint activities extremely useful. The good news is that these activities can be extended to produce an extensive range of attractive classroom resources.

Key features to help you progress easily include:

- Teacher/Adult ICT Skills Activity Checklist;
- A 'How to....' getting started guide;
- Early Learning Goals checklist;
- National Literacy and Numeracy Strategy objectives.

The CD ROM that accompanies *Great ICT Ideas for Early Years and Key Stage 1 Teachers* contains all of the files you need to get great results.

client ✓

ICT, Literacy & Numeracy

Word

How to create resources using Word

How to add Clip Art to your document

1. Click on **Insert**.

2. Click on **Picture**.

3. Click on **Clip Art**.

4. Click on the picture that you wish to use.

5. Click on **Insert**.

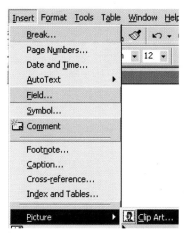

To change the size

1. Click on your picture.

2. Holding down the left mouse button drag the handles in or out to make the picture larger or smaller.

To change the position

1. Click on the picture.

2. Point to the middle of the picture and holding the left mouse button down drag the picture to its new position.

To add graphics saved on file to your document

1. Click on **Insert**.

2. Click on **Picture**.

3. Click on **From File**.

4. Select the folder in which you have saved the graphic.

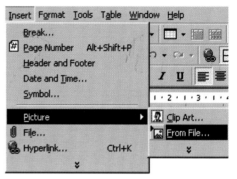

5. Click on the graphic file that you wish to use.

6. Click on **Insert**.

How to add Text Boxes

Text boxes are useful if you wish to place text in a particular place e.g. next to a picture.

1. Click on **Insert** and then **Text Box**. A symbol similar to a plus sign will appear.

2. Hold down the left mouse button and drag the mouse to increase / decrease the size of the box.

This text is inside a TextBox

3. Type your text in the Text Box.

 client ✓

Adding graphics and text boxes

Word

To colour a Text Box

1. Click on the Text Box.

2. Click on the **Fill Color** icon on the drawing tool bar.

3. To select a different colour click on the down arrow next to the **Fill Color** icon and click on the colour of your choice.

To add **to your document**

1. Click on **Insert** and then **Picture**.

2. Click on **WordArt** and select the style you would like to use.

3. Click on **OK**.

4. Choose the font style and size you want to use.

5. Type in your text and click on **OK**.

To open the Drawing toolbar (if not already open)

1. Click on **View** and then **Toolbars**.

2. Select **Drawing**. The drawing toolbar will now appear at the bottom of the screen.

To add AutoShapes

1. Click on the **AutoShapes** button.   AutoShapes ▼

2. Click on the type of shape you would like e.g. **Basic Shapes**.

3. Click on a shape of your choice.

4. Hold down the left mouse button and drag the mouse to increase / decrease the size of the shape.

To rotate an AutoShape

1. Click on the shape you wish to rotate.

2. Click on the **Free Rotate** icon.

3. Point to a green spot that appears on the edge of your shape.

4. Hold down your left mouse button whilst you drag the shape to rotate it.

Drawing toolbar and AutoShapes

Word

To add shadow to an AutoShape

1. Click on the shape you wish to add shadow to.

2. Click on the **Shadow** icon.

To colour an Autoshape

1. Click on the AutoShape.

2. Click on the **Fill Color** icon on the drawing tool bar.

To select a different colour click on the down arrow next to the **Fill Color** icon and click on the colour of your choice.

To draw lines

1. Click on the **Line** icon.

2. Click where you want to start drawing and keeping the mouse button held down drag the mouse to increase / decrease the size of the line.

3. Release the mouse button and the line will appear.

4. To change the thickness or line style of your line click on the **Line Style** or **Dash Style** icon and click on the style of your choice.

To add Arrows to your document

1. Click on the **Arrow** icon on the drawing tool bar.

2. Click where you want to start drawing the arrow and, keeping the mouse button held down, move to where you want the arrow to point.

3. Release the mouse button and the arrow will appear.

4. To change the style of arrow click on the **Arrow Style** icon on the drawing tool bar and click on the arrow of your choice.

To animate text

1. Enter your text.

2. Highlight the text you wish to animate.

3. Click on **Format** and then **Font**.

4. Click on the **Text Effects** or **Animation** tab.

5. Click on an animation from the list e.g. **Sparkle Text**.

6. Click on **OK**.

client ✓

Adding arrows and animating text

PowerPoint

How to create PowerPoint presentations

To create a presentation

1. Click on **Blank Presentation** and click on **OK**.

2. Click on **AutoLayout** of your choice and click on **OK**.

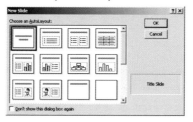

To create a background

1. Click on **Format** and then click on **Background**.

2. Click on the down arrow and then click on **Fill Effects**.

3. Select background from **Gradient, Pattern, Texture** or **Picture** tabs and click on **OK**.

NB: You can also create your own background by adding a picture from Clip Art and stretching it to fill the entire slide (see below).

To apply a Design Template

1. Click on **Format** and then **Apply Design Template**.

2. Click on the template design of your choice e.g. **Sunny Days** and click on **OK**.

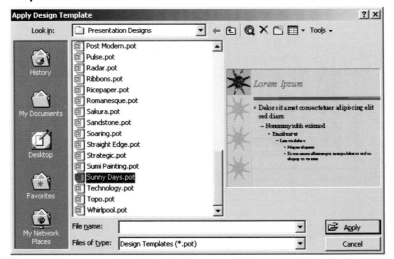

To open the Drawing toolbar (if not open)

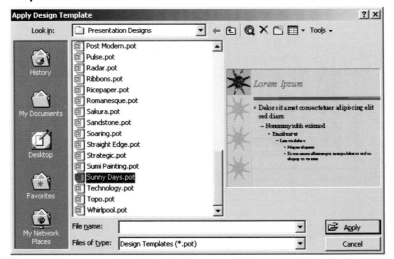

1. Click on **View** and then **Toolbars**.

2. Select **Drawing**. The drawing toolbar will now appear at the bottom of the screen.

PowerPoint

To add AutoShapes

1. Click on the **AutoShapes** button.

2. Click on the type of shape you would like e.g. **Basic Shapes**.

3. Click on a shape of your choice.

4. Hold down the left mouse button and drag the mouse to increase or decrease the size of the shape.

To add Clip Art

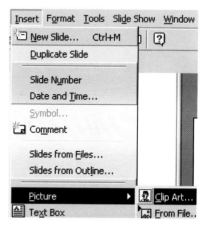

1. Click on **Insert** and then click on **Picture**.

2. Click on **Clip Art**.

3. Click on the picture that you wish to use and then click on **Insert**.

To copy graphics from another document

1. Point to the graphic (picture) you wish to copy.

2. Right click the mouse and click on **Copy**.

3. Open the document you wish to paste the graphic into.

4. Click on **Edit** and then **Paste**.

Edit	View	Insert	Format
⤺ Can't Undo		Ctrl+Z
↻ Repeat		Ctrl+Y
✂ Cut		Ctrl+X
📋 Copy		Ctrl+C
📋 Paste		Ctrl+V
Paste Special...		
Paste as Hyperlink		
Clear		Del
Select All		Ctrl+A
Duplicate		Ctrl+D
Delete Slide		
🔍 Find...		Ctrl+F
Replace...		Ctrl+H
Go to Property...		
Links...		
Object		

To add Text Boxes

Text boxes are useful if you wish to place text or clip art in a particular place.

1. Click on **Insert** and then **Text Box**. A symbol similar to a plus sign will appear.

2. Hold down the left mouse button and drag the mouse to increase / decrease the size of the box.

This text is inside a TextBox

client ✓

Copying graphics and adding text boxes

PowerPoint

To animate text or Clip Art

1. Click on the Text Box or Clip Art you want to animate.

2. Click on **Slide Show** and **Custom Animation**.

3. On **Effects** tab click on animation of your choice e.g. **Dissolve** and click on **OK**.

To create sound effects

1. Click on the Text Box or Clip Art you want to add sound to.

2. Click on **Slide Show** and **Custom Animation**.

3. On **Effects** tab click on sound of your choice e.g. **Clapping** and click on **OK**.

To insert a new slide

1. Click on **Insert** and then **New Slide**.

2. Choose one of the **AutoLayouts** shown.

3. Click on **OK**.

To run your presentation

1. Click on **Slide Show** and **View Show**.

2. Click to animate text or clip art.

client ✓

Inserting a new slide

Literacy
Using Word

ICT & Communication, Language and Literacy - Using Word

Teacher ICT Skills Activity Checklist Activity:	CD ROM File	Load Word	Add WordArt	Add Clip Art	Add Text Boxes	Colour Text Boxes	Add arrows
Find the sound	L01	*	*				
Find the letter	L02	*		*	*		
At words	L03	*	*		*		
Rhyming words	L04	*	*				*
Matching pictures	L05	*	*	*			*
Alphabet	L06	*	*		*	*	
Make a sentence	L07	*	*		*	*	
Matching letters	L08	*			*	*	*
Matching words	L09	*			*	*	*
Matching words & pictures	L10	*		*	*	*	*

Activity 1: Find the sound

Introduction

This 'Find the sound' matching game is designed to encourage the children to identify specific vowel sounds but when simple changes are made to the file, it can be used for any sounds. Individually or in pairs, the children either underline or circle the 'o' sounds in the words on the page or on the Interactive Whiteboard.

Take the opportunity to use this simple technique to create lots of useful resources which are ideal for a busy Early Years classroom.

Learning objectives

Early Learning Goals for Communication, Language and Literacy:

- Enjoy listening to and using spoken and written language.

National Literacy Strategy Objectives:

Word Level
- Reading letter(s) that represent(s) the sound(s);
- Using knowledge of rhyme to identify families of rhyming CVC words.

client ✓

Activity 1: Find the sound

Literacy
Using Word

More ideas!

As an extension to the 'Find the sound' activity described, you may wish to ask the children to complete one or more of the following:

- Identify other words containing the 'o' sound;
- Make a collection of objects or pictures of items;
- Draw pictures of items containing the 'o' sound;
- Label pictures of items containing the 'o' sound.

Find the 'o' sound

Underline the 'o' words

cat	fog	bun
pot	tin	hat
dog	mat	win
sun	cot	fed
pin	fun	rod

CD ROM: L01

Activity 2: Find the letter

Introduction

'Find the letter' consists of CVC words with the last letter missing. The pictures are clues for the children and the possible endings are contained in text boxes in a row on the page. The children can either drag the letter to the end of the incomplete word or insert the missing letter by typing it in the available space. The children can either work individually, in pairs or groups.

This file can be easily adapted to reflect the relevant needs of the children. By substituting the words and pictures, endless useful resources can be created.

Learning objectives

Early Learning Goals for Communication, Language and Literacy:

- Enjoy listening to and using spoken and written language;
- Hear and say initial and final sounds in words;
- Link sounds to letters, naming and sounding the letters of the alphabet;
- Use their phonic knowledge to write simple regular words and make phonetically plausible attempts at more complex words.

client ✓

Literacy

Using Word

National Literacy Strategy Objectives:

> **Word Level**
> * Reading letter(s) that represent(s) the sound(s);
> * Identifying and writing initial and final phonemes in CVC words;
> * Using knowledge of rhyme to identify families of rhyming CVC words.

More ideas!

* Identifying alternative endings for each word;
* Identifying other words which end with the same letter;
* Make a collection of objects which end with the same letter;
* Draw pictures of objects ending with the same letter;
* Label pictures ending with the same letter.

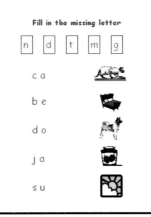

CD ROM: L02

Activity 3: 'at' words

Introduction

How many words can you make from words that end with 'at'? Identifying a range of different words that have the same ending helps the children increase their knowledge and understanding of word formation and word patterns. Working individually, in pairs or small groups children add the initial letters to create a list of rhyming words.

This activity can also be adapted to explore any group of rhyming CVC words.

Learning objectives

Early Learning Goals for Communication, Language and Literacy:

- Enjoy listening to and using spoken and written language;
- Hear and say initial and final sounds in words;
- Link sounds to letters, naming and sounding the letters of the alphabet.

client✓

National Literacy Strategy Objectives:

> **Word Level**
> - Recognising, exploring and working with rhyming patterns;
> - Hearing and identifying initial sounds in words;
> - Reading letter(s) that represent(s) the sound(s);
> - Identifying and writing initial and final phonemes in CVC words;
> - Using knowledge of rhyme to identify families of rhyming CVC words.

More ideas!

- Identify other words ending in 'at';
- Draw pictures of objects within the 'at' word family;
- Label pictures of objects within the 'at' word family;
- Make a collection of 'at' objects.

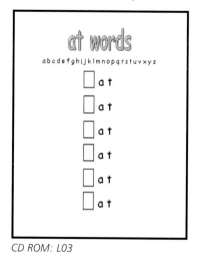

CD ROM: L03

Activity 4: Rhyming words

Introduction

Match the 'Rhyming words' using online tools or a pencil and paper. This simple activity requires the children to draw arrows between to link the words that rhyme. The children may complete this activity individually or in pairs.

You can also substitute the words used to reflect the work currently being undertaken by the children.

Learning objectives

Early Learning Goals for Communication, Language and Literacy:

- Enjoy listening to and using spoken and written language;
- Hear and say initial and final sounds in words;
- Link sounds to letters, naming and sounding the letters of the alphabet.

client ✓

Activity 4: Rhyming words

National Literacy Strategy Objectives:

Word Level
- Recognising, exploring and working with rhyming patterns;
- Reading letter(s) that represent(s) the sound(s);
- Using knowledge of rhyme to identify families of rhyming CVC words;
- Read on sight a range of familiar words.

More ideas!

- Identifying other rhyming words;
- Drawing pictures of objects which have names that rhyme;
- Labelling pictures of objects that rhyme;
- Suggesting sentences within which each word would fit.

Rhyming words

Join the words that rhyme with an arrow

cat	fog	bun
red	tin	hat
pin	fun	log
dog	mat	fed
sun	bed	win

CD ROM: L04

Activity 5: Matching pictures

Introduction

'Matching pictures' provides the children with the opportunity to look for images that look the same and have the same name. This activity can be completed by individual children or by children taking turns whilst working in pairs. It can also be used with an Interactive Whiteboard.

By changing the pictures to be matched, the activity can be linked to work that is being undertaken in the classroom generally.

Learning objectives

Early Learning Goals for Communication, Language and Literacy:

*   Enjoy listening to and using spoken and written language.

client ✓

Activity 5: Matching pictures

More ideas!

- Find matching pairs of real objects;
- Explore matching within other contexts e.g. playing games of snap;
- Label the pictures;
- Match letters of the alphabet and CVC words.

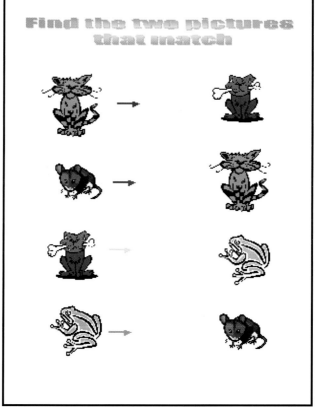

CD ROM: L05

Activity 6: Alphabet

Introduction

By putting the correct letters in the right order, the children can see how the alphabet is formed. This is a simple activity designed to be completed by children on an individual basis. Children click in the text box and type in the relevant letter of the alphabet.

A series of pictures or objects that correspond to each letter of the alphabet could also be created as additional support for the children.

Learning objectives

Early Learning Goals for Communication, Language and Literacy:

- Enjoy listening to and using spoken and written language.

National Literacy Strategy Objectives:

Word Level
- Reading letter(s) that represent(s) the sound(s);
- Using knowledge of rhyme to identify families of rhyming CVC words.

client ✓

More ideas!

- Recite the letters of the alphabet in order;
- Draw pictures to illustrate each letter of the alphabet;
- Create an alphabet frieze with pictures for each letter of the alphabet;
- Create a class alphabet book or dictionary.

CD ROM: L06

Activity 7: Make a sentence

Introduction

This activity is designed for the children to work individually, in pairs or small groups. The aim here is to 'Make a sentence'. **'This is my** . . . ' is repeated at the beginning of each new sentence and by dragging the text boxes into position within the on-screen sentence maker boxes, the last word in the sentence makes it complete.

Many different words within the text boxes can be substituted so that the resource can be used again and again.

Learning objectives

Early Learning Goals for Communication, Language and Literacy:

- Enjoy listening to and using spoken and written language;
- Read a range of familiar and common words and simple sentences independently;
- Know that print carries meaning, and in English is read from left to right and top to bottom;
- Attempt writing for various purposes.

Literacy
Using Word

National Literacy Strategy Objectives:

> **Word Level**
> - Read on sight a range of familiar words;
>
> **Sentence Level**
> - Use awareness of the grammar of a sentence to predict words during shared reading;
> - Words are ordered left to right and need to be read that way to make sense;
>
> **Text Level**
> - Use writing to communicate in a variety of ways.

More ideas!

- Use clip art or a drawing package to illustrate their sentences;
- Create and illustrate a book using their sentences;
- Suggest and record (if appropriate) alternative endings for 'This is my . . .' sentences;
- Explore other sentences which follow a pattern e.g. 'I like my . . .'

CD ROM: L07

Activity 8: Matching letters

Introduction

By drawing an arrow using the on-screen drawing tools or by using pencil and paper, the children are encouraged to recognise and bring together letters that are matching pairs. The ability to differentiate between some letters may require additional support from an adult.

The letters can be replaced with different ones in order to meet individual or group needs.

Learning objectives

Early Learning Goals for Communication, Language and Literacy:

- Enjoy listening to and using spoken and written language.

National Literacy Strategy Objectives:

Word Level
• Reading letter(s) that represent(s) the sound(s).

client ✓

More ideas!

- Explore other matching pairs of letters;
- Use Clip Art or a drawing package to illustrate these letters of the alphabet;
- Match upper and lower case letters of the alphabet;
- Explore matching within other contexts.

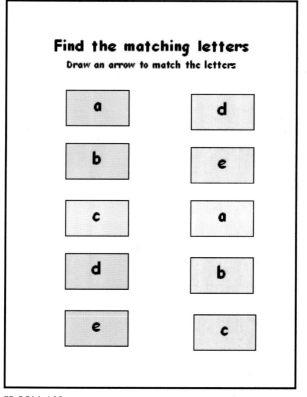

CD ROM: L08

Activity 9: Matching words

Introduction

This 'Matching words' activity is for completion by individual children, pairs or it can be used for whole class teaching. The arrows to join the words can either be created on-screen or by using pencil and paper.
Each of the guesses made by the children can be saved or the action taken, reversed at the click of the mouse, as and when necessary. An Interactive Whiteboard can also be used to enhance this activity.

Substitute the words used and endless files can be created and used again and again.

Learning objectives

Early Learning Goals for Communication, Language and Literacy:

- Enjoy listening to and using spoken and written language.

National Literacy Strategy Objectives:

> **Word Level**
> - Read on sight a range of familiar words.

client ✓

More ideas!

- Explore other matching pairs of words;
- Use Clip Art or a drawing package to illustrate these words;
- Create a class display with labels;
- Label pictures on screen using these words.

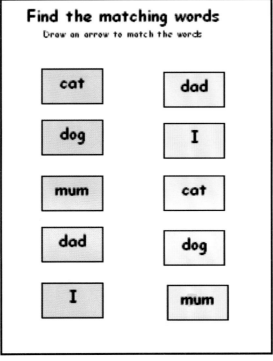

Find the matching words

Draw an arrow to match the words

cat	dad
dog	I
mum	cat
dad	dog
I	mum

CD ROM: L09

Activity 10: Matching words & pictures

Introduction

By simply joining the words and the pictures on screen using the drawing tools or on paper, the children can combine images and text that match. It is also possible to drag the words to the right picture by using the mouse.

This technique can be used when working with a group of children or the whole class.

Learning objectives

Early Learning Goals for Communication, Language and Literacy:

- Enjoy listening to and using spoken and written language.

National Literacy Strategy Objectives:

> **Word Level**
> - Read on sight a range of familiar words.

client ✓ **Activity 10: Matching words & pictures**

Literacy
Using Word

More ideas!

- Write their own labels for pictures;
- Draw their own pictures to illustrate key words;
- Suggest a sentence within which each word would fit;
- Create a simple 'words and pictures' book.

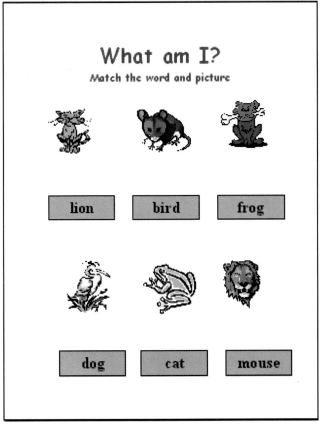

CD ROM: L10

ICT & Communication, Language and Literacy - Using PowerPoint

Teacher ICT Skills Activity Checklist Activity:	CD ROM File	Load PowerPoint	Choose an Autolayout	Add a Background	Apply a Design Template	Add Clip Art	Animate Clip Art & AutoShapes	Add Text Boxes	Animate text	Add images from other documents	Add sound effects	Add a new slide	Run the presentation
Letter to Santa	L11	*	*	*		*							*
All about us	L12	*	*		*							*	*
Labels and captions	L13	*	*			*	*					*	*
Humpty Dumpty	L14	*	*	*				*	*				*
Frog story	L15	*	*						*			*	*
A is for	L16	*	*	*		*	*				*		*
Letters and sounds	L17	*	*		*	*	*	*	*				*
Rhyming words	L18	*	*	*		*		*			*		*
Snow	L19	*	*			*		*	*		*		*
Goldilocks	L20	*	*		*	*	*	*			*	*	*

Activity 11: Letter to Santa

Introduction

Writing letters at any time of the year can be great fun. This 'Letter to Santa' activity is a good starting point for encouraging children to write for different purposes.

By using a template, the children can work individually, in groups or as a whole class and lots of changes can be easily made to meet individual needs. Some children will also be able to work independently and record their own ideas; others may require additional support or help from a Word Bank.

The 'Letter to Santa' template can be adopted for use within other contexts.

Learning objectives

Early Learning Goals for Communication, Language and Literacy:

- Enjoy listening to and using spoken and written language;
- Know that print carries meaning, and in English is read from left to right and top to bottom;
- Attempt writing for various purposes;
- Write their own names and other things such as labels and captions and begin to form simple sentences, sometimes using punctuation;

- Use their phonic knowledge to write simple regular words and make phonetically plausible attempts at more complex words.

National Literacy Strategy Objectives:

Word Level
- Read and write own name;

Sentence Level
- Use a capital letter for the start of their own name;

Text Level
- Write their own names;
- Use writing to communicate in a variety of ways.

More ideas!
- Write a letter to a friend;
- Share the children's presentations with another class;
- Make a display of the children's work;
- Explore letter writing in role-play.

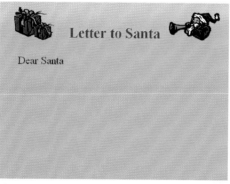

Letter to Santa

Dear Santa

CD ROM: L11

Activity 12: All about us

Introduction

'All about us' will help the children experience writing using their phonic knowledge. Some children will be able to describe themselves in sentences and others may choose to use their name and individual words only. You can easily create a whole-class presentation with the children and every child can take part. The children can also use the mouse button to advance each page as they take turns to present their 'All about us' presentations to each other, other classes or parents.

A Word Bank can also help children that need additional support.

Learning objectives

Early Learning Goals for Communication, Language and Literacy:

- Attempt writing for a variety of purposes;
- Write their own name and other things such as captions;
- Use phonic knowledge to write simple regular words and make phonetically plausible attempts at more complex words.

client ✓

Literacy
Using PowerPoint

National Literacy Strategy Objectives:

Word Level
- Read and write own name;

Sentence Level
- Use a capital letter for the start of their own name;

Text Level
- Write their own names;
- Use writing to communicate in a variety of ways.

More ideas!

- Create a presentation with a particular focus e.g. pets, food;
- Create a picture gallery using a drawing package;
- Make a collection of special objects;
- Use a digital camera to take pictures for the presentations.

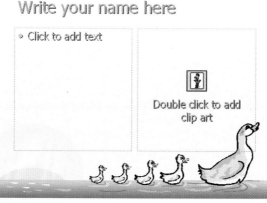

CD ROM: L12

Activity 13: Labels and captions

Introduction

The 'Labels and captions' activity will allow the children to work individually or in pairs. It can also be used as a whole-class activity. The pictures are easily identifiable and will be familiar to the children. They can either insert a single word that identifies the picture or create more words to describe it generally, e.g. dog, black, big, fluffy. More complex words and sentences can be created when working with children of different ability levels.

Once the children have completed labelling or inserting their captions they could present their ideas to each other, and explain their choice of words.

Learning objectives

Early Learning Goals for Communication, Language and Literacy:

- Attempt writing for a variety of purposes;
- Write things such as labels and captions and begin to form simple sentences, sometimes using punctuation;
- Use their phonic knowledge to write simple regular words and make phonetically plausible attempts at more complex words.

National Literacy Strategy Objectives:

Text Level
- Use writing to communicate in a variety of ways;
- Write labels or captions for pictures.

More ideas!

- Write labels or captions for a variety of objects around the classroom;
- Add pre-selected pictures to pre-prepared labels or captions;
- Match pictures and labels on screen.

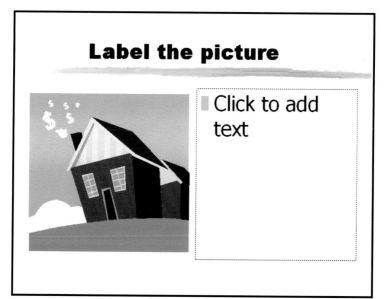

CD ROM: L13

Activity 14: Humpty Dumpty

Introduction

The 'Humpty Dumpty' nursery rhyme is well known and loved by children. Each time you or the children click the mouse, a new line in the rhyme appears. When read aloud, the pace of the rhyme is controlled.

Lots of different extension activities can be created using Humpty Dumpty. You can leave spaces for 'missing words' or substitute words for pictures e.g. wall, horses, men.

This idea could be adapted for use with other nursery rhymes or verses.

Learning objectives

Early Learning Goals for Communication, Language and Literacy:

- Enjoy listening to and using spoken and written language;
- Listen with enjoyment and respond to rhymes;
- Use language to imagine and recreate roles and experiences;
- Know that print carries meaning and, in English, is read from left to right and top to bottom.

National Literacy Strategy Objectives:

Word Level
- Read on sight a range of familiar words;
- Explore new words from their reading and experiences;

Sentence Level
- Use awareness of the grammar of a sentence to predict words during shared reading and when re-reading familiar stories;
- Words are ordered left to right and need to be read that way to make sense;

Text Level
- Use a variety of cues when reading;
- Use writing to communicate in a variety of ways.

More ideas!
- Select their own nursery rhyme to present to others;
- Create a picture using a drawing package;
- Amend this or compose their own nursery rhyme (as a class);
- Record the class reciting Humpty Dumpty.

Humpty Dumpty

Humpty Dumpty sat on the wall,
Humpty Dumpty had a great fall.
All the King's horses
And all the King's men,
Couldn't put Humpty together again.

CD ROM: L14

Activity 15: Frog story

Introduction

Re-tell this simple story time and time again by adding different text to the colourful images. The children can work individually, in groups or this could also be used as a whole-class activity. The pictures provide an excellent visual stimulus for the many different stories that can be created by the children.

Presenting the completed stories to a group or the whole class will show just how different each story can be. Clicking the mouse button will advance each page and the stories can be read aloud by the author or authors.

Learning objectives

Early Learning Goals for Communication, Language and Literacy:

- Re-tell narratives in the correct sequences, drawing on the language patterns of stories;
- Show an understanding of the elements of stories;
- Attempt writing for a variety of purposes;
- Use phonic knowledge to write simple regular words and make phonetically plausible attempts at more complex words.

client ✓

National Literacy Strategy Objectives:

Text Level
- Understand how story book language works;
- To re-read and recite stories and rhymes;
- Write labels or captions for pictures;
- Write sentences to match pictures or sequences of pictures;
- Use experience of stories as a basis for independent writing;
- Use writing to communicate in a variety of ways.

More ideas!
- Discuss what 'might' have happened next in the story;
- Use a drawing package to create illustrations to show what may have happened next;
- Use a tape recorder to record their version of the story;
- Re-enact the story through role-play or dance.

The frog story

CD ROM: L15

Activity 16: 'a' is for

Introduction

Whether you are working with the whole class or a group of children, this activity has endless possibilities. At the click of the mouse, a picture that begins with the letter 'a' is revealed. As each object appears, the children name it. Before they start, they could guess what they think will appear! Many more letters of the alphabet can be added to this slide and a whole alphabet slide show can be simply created and used again and again.

Learning objectives

Early Learning Goals for Communication, Language and Literacy:

- Explore and experiment with sounds;
- Hear and say initial sounds in words;
- Link sounds to letters, naming and sounding the letters of the alphabet.

client ✓

National Literacy Strategy Objectives:

Word Level
- Hear and identify initial sounds in words;
- Read letter(s) that represent(s) the sound(s);
- Sound and name each letter of the alphabet.

Text Level
- Use writing to communicate in a variety of ways.

More ideas!
- Name additional items that begin with the letter 'a';
- Make a collection of items;
- Draw or paint pictures of things that begin with a specific letter of the alphabet;
- Cut out and keep a collection of images from magazines;
- Label a set of pictures or items to create an alphabet matching game.

CD ROM: L16

Activity 17: Letters and sounds

Introduction

In 'Letters and sounds', one object is revealed at a time on the click of the mouse. The children, working in groups or as a whole class, name the objects as they appear. Finally, the letter that corresponds with the initial letter of each of the words is revealed.

You can add other slides to this presentation and explore lots more letters and sounds with the children.

Learning objectives

Early Learning Goals for Communication, Language and Literacy:

- Explore and experiment with sounds;
- Hear and say initial sounds in words;
- Link sounds to letters, naming and sounding the letters of the alphabet.

National Literacy Strategy Objectives:

> **Word Level**
> - Hear and identify initial sounds in words;
> - Read letter(s) that represent(s) the sound(s);
> - Sound and name each letter of the alphabet.
>
> **Text Level**
> - Use writing to communicate in a variety of ways.

More ideas!

- Identify additional objects beginning with 'c' e.g. in the house, in the garden;
- Make a class collection of objects that begin with the same sound and are made from the same material;
- Cut out pictures of objects;
- Draw or label objects;
- Use a drawing package to create pictures of objects.

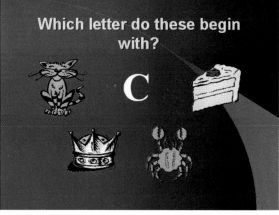

CD ROM: L17

Activity 18: Rhyming words

Introduction

The introduction of rhyming words using PowerPoint makes simple CVC words come alive and helps the children remember sound patterns and word shapes. This activity is designed for whole class or group work. Either the teacher or the pupil can click the mouse button to reveal one word at a time. By reading the words aloud this creates the stimulus for discussion and written work.

Learning objectives

Early Learning Goals for Communication, Language and Literacy:

- Enjoy listening to and using spoken and written language;
- Explore and experiment with sounds and words;
- Extend their vocabulary, exploring the meanings and sounds of new words;
- Hear and say initial and final sounds in words;
- Link sounds to letters.

client ✓

Literacy
Using PowerPoint

National Literacy Strategy Objectives:

Word Level
- Recognising, exploring and working with rhyming patterns;
- Hearing and identifying initial sounds in words;
- Reading letter(s) that represent(s) the sound(s);
- Identifying and writing initial and final phonemes in CVC words;
- Using knowledge of rhyme to identify families of rhyming CVC words;
- Read on sight a range of familiar words;
- Explore new words from their reading and experiences;

Text Level
- Use writing to communicate in a variety of ways.

More ideas!
- Identify a sentence in which one or more of the rhyming words fits;
- Draw pictures of these objects;
- Label pictures of objects that rhyme;
- Explore other families of rhyming words;
- Identify pairs of rhyming words within nursery rhymes.

Rhyming words		
Join the words that rhyme with an arrow		
cat	fog	bun
red	tin	hat
pin	fun	log
dog	mat	fed
sun	bed	win

CD ROM: L18

More ideas!

57

Activity 19: Snow

Introduction

Here you will find that words describing the snow are revealed at the click of the mouse and many more slides can be easily created to develop the children's vocabulary. The visual impact of the scene can be explored and discussed and particular letters can be used to complement the scene e.g. Snow is crisp, clear, cold; Snow is wonderful, white, wet.

This idea could be adapted for use within a wide range of topics surrounding, for example, the seasons, pets, transport, holidays.

Learning objectives

Early Learning Goals for Communication, Language and Literacy:

- Enjoy listening to and using spoken and written language;
- Explore and experiment with words and texts;
- Extend their vocabulary, exploring the meanings and sounds of new words.

client ✓

National Literacy Strategy Objectives:

Word Level
- Identifying alliteration in known and new and invented words;
- Explore new words from their reading and shared experiences;
- Make collections of words linked to particular topics.

Text Level
- Use writing to communicate in a variety of ways.

More ideas!
- Suggest other words which describe snow;
- Identify a sentence in which each word fits;
- Create a 'snowy' picture using a drawing package;
- Record their own 'snowy' words on screen.

CD ROM: L19

Activity 20: Goldilocks

Introduction

This simple activity is designed for whole class or group work. The teacher or pupil clicks the mouse button to reveal the pictures and text within the story. The teacher reads the story to the children and / or they read the story aloud together.

Such a story could be one the class have written together or could provide a model for such work.

Learning objectives

Early Learning Goals for Communication, Language and Literacy:

- Enjoy listening to and using spoken and written language;
- Explore and experiment with texts;
- Listen with enjoyment and respond to stories and make up their own stories;
- Show an understanding of the elements of stories.

National Literacy Strategy Objectives:

Word Level
- Read on sight a range of familiar words;
- Explore new words from their reading and experiences;

Sentence Level:
- Use awareness of the grammar of a sentence to predict words during shared reading and when re-reading familiar stories;
- Words are ordered left to right and need to be read that way to make sense;

Text Level
- Use a variety of cues when reading;
- Understand how story book language works;
- To re-read and recite stories and rhymes;
- Use writing to communicate in a variety of ways.

More ideas!
- Suggest what happened next in the story;
- Write their own version of the Goldilocks story on screen;
- Use a drawing package to create a picture of Goldilocks;
- Explore the story through role-play.

CD ROM: L20

ICT & Numeracy and Mathematical Development - Using Word

Teacher ICT Skills Activity Checklist Activity:	CD ROM File	Load Word	Add WordArt	Add Clip Art	Add AutoShapes	Colour AutoShapes	Add Text Boxes	Colour Text Boxes	Add lines	Animate text
Tallest and shortest	N21	*		*						
How many	N22	*					*			
Number order	N23	*					*	*		
Matching numbers	N24	*	*	*			*	*		
Sorting shapes	N25	*	*		*	*				
Sorting colours	N26	*	*		*	*				
Favourite colours	N27	*	*		*	*			*	
Continue the pattern	N28	*	*		*	*			*	
Take away	N29	*	*	*			*		*	
Can you count	N30	*		*			*			*

Activity 21:Tallest and shortest

Introduction

This activity invites the children to place the objects in order of size. They need to drag and drop the items into the correct position on screen.

Similar activities could be created which explore concepts such as long and short.

Learning objectives

Early Learning Goals for Mathematical Development:

- Use language such as 'circle' or 'bigger' to describe the shape and size of solids and flat shapes.

National Numeracy Strategy Objectives:

Measures, shape and space
- Put sets of objects in order of size.

More ideas!

- Explore size order using real objects e.g. 'Compare bears';
- Draw their own objects in order of size;
- Label objects 'tallest' and 'shortest';
- Explore related concepts such 'long' and 'short'.

CD ROM: N21

Activity 22: How many?

Introduction

This activity introduces the children to the concept of addition. The children add up the total number of items shown and then record the total in the text box provided.

Such an activity could be adapted to explore further addition problems including number bonds.

Learning objectives

Early Learning Goals for Mathematical Development:

- Say and use number names in order in familiar contexts;
- Count reliably up to 10 everyday objects;
- Recognise numerals 1 to 9;
- Begin to relate addition to combining two groups of objects, and subtraction to 'taking away'.

National Numeracy Strategy Objectives:

Counting and recognising numbers
- Say and use number names in order in familiar contexts;
- Recite the number names in order, continuing the count forwards or backwards from a given number;

client ✓

- Count reliably up to 10 everyday objects;
- Recognise numerals 1 to 9;

Adding and subtracting
- Begin to relate addition to combining two groups of objects;
- Begin to relate addition to counting on.

More ideas!

- Explore combining groups of real objects;
- Find the total of two numbers up to 10;
- Write the number of objects shown in each group as well as the total;
- Draw the number of objects shown in numerals.

How many altogether?

1 and 3 makes ☐

2 and 4 makes ☐

3 and 2 makes ☐

4 and 1 makes ☐

CD ROM: N22

Activity 23: Number order

Introduction

This activity challenges the children's understanding of place value. The children need to drag the text boxes around the screen to position them in the correct order.

This activity could be adapted simply by replacing the numbers currently shown within the text boxes.

Learning objectives

Early Learning Goals for Mathematical Development:

- Say and use number names in order in familiar contexts;
- Count reliably up to 10 everyday objects;
- Recognise numerals 1 to 9.

National Numeracy Strategy Objectives:

Counting and recognising numbers
- Say and use number names in order in familiar contexts;
- Recognise numerals 1 to 9;
- Order a given set of numbers.

client ✓

More ideas!

- Identify hidden numbers within a number line;
- Enter missing numbers within a number line;
- Draw objects to illustrate the number shown;
- Create a class number frieze / display.

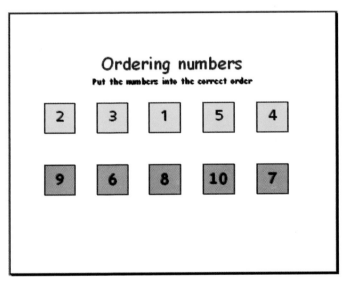

CD ROM: N23

Activity 24: Matching numbers

Introduction

Within this activity children are asked to draw an arrow between each numeral (or digit) shown and the corresponding number of items.

Similar activities could be created which ask children to match e.g. colours or shapes and their names.

Learning objectives

Early Learning Goals for Mathematical Development:

- Say and use number names in order in familiar contexts;
- Count reliably up to 10 everyday objects;
- Recognise numerals 1 to 9.

National Numeracy Strategy Objectives:

Counting and recognising numbers:
- Say and use number names in order in familiar contexts;
- Recognise numerals 1 to 9.

More ideas!

- Match numbers up to 10;
- Create a numbers to 5 (or 10) zigzag book;
- Fill in the number of items shown on screen;
- Draw the number of items shown on screen.

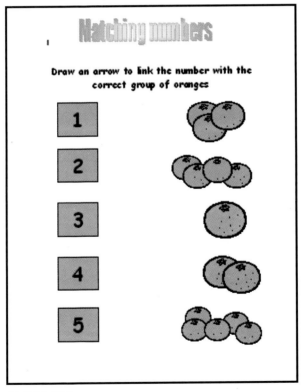

CD ROM: N24

Activity 25: Sorting shapes

Introduction

Within this activity children explore circles and squares by dragging them into the appropriate set.

This idea could be adapted by replacing these shapes with other autoshapes or clip art for children to sort into groups.

Learning objectives

Early Learning Goals for Mathematical Development:

- Use language such as 'circle' or 'bigger' to describe the shape and size of solids and flat shapes.

National Numeracy Strategy Objectives:

> **Solving problems**
> - Sort and match objects;
>
> **Measures, shape and space:**
> - Use language such as circle or bigger to describe the shape and size of solids and flat shapes.

client ✓

Numeracy

Using Word

More ideas!

- Sort 2D shapes practically;
- Draw simple 2D shapes in the appropriate sets;
- Label simple 2D shapes on screen;
- Create simple pictures using 2D shapes on screen.

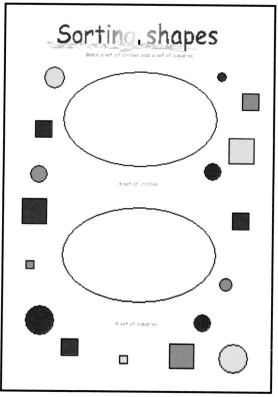

CD ROM: N25

Activity 26: Sorting colours

Introduction

This is a simple activity in which the children drag the coloured shapes into the appropriate set.

By merely replacing the text underneath each of these sets, the activity could be used to sort shapes. The shapes could also be replaced by clip art which children could be asked to sort in a variety of ways.

Learning objectives

Early Learning Goals for Mathematical Development:

- Use language such as 'circle' or 'bigger' to describe the shape and size of solids and flat shapes.

National Numeracy Strategy Objectives:

> **Solving problems**
> - Sort and match objects.

More ideas!

- Sort coloured shapes / objects within practical activities;
- Colour the shapes / objects shown on screen appropriately;
- Label shapes / objects shown on screen according to their colour;
- Create repeating patterns of shapes / objects.

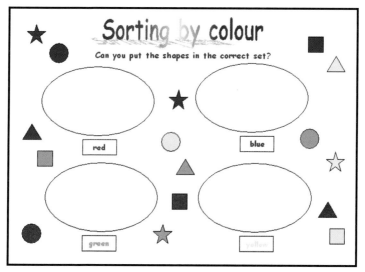

CD ROM: N26

Activity 27: Favourite colours

Introduction

This data handling activity will allow the children to record their favourite colours to build up a chart of children's favourite colours. Individual children can copy and paste the coloured blocks, placing them in position on the axis provided.

Similar activities could be created using clip art whereby children record favourite foods, animals etc.

Learning objectives

Early Learning Goals for Mathematical Development:

- Say and use number names in order in familiar contexts;
- Count reliably up to 10 everyday objects;
- Recognise numerals 1 to 9.

National Numeracy Strategy Objectives:

Counting and recognising numbers:
- Say and use number names in order in familiar contexts;
- Recognise numerals 1 to 9.

More ideas!

- Create a 3D chart using real objects e.g. cubes;
- Use clip art to create a pictogram;
- Use tables to record childrens data handling activities;
- Create charts to record other data handling activities.

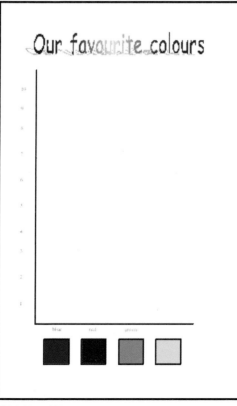

CD ROM: N27

Activity 28: Continue the pattern

Introduction

This activity promotes colour recognition and pattern recognition.   Individually or in pairs, the children continue the pattern of colours shown. They do this by copying and pasting the beads in the correct sequence.

A similar activity could be created where children continue a pattern of shapes.

Learning objectives

Early Learning Goals for Mathematical Development:

- Talk about, recognise and recreate simple patterns.

National Numeracy Strategy Objectives:

Solving problems
- Talk about, recognise and recreate simple patterns;

Measures, shape and space
- Talk about, recognise and recreate patterns.

client ✓

More ideas!

- Explore repeating patterns using real objects e.g. beads;
- Continue a pattern of shapes;
- Explore more complex repeating patterns;
- Create their own repeating patterns.

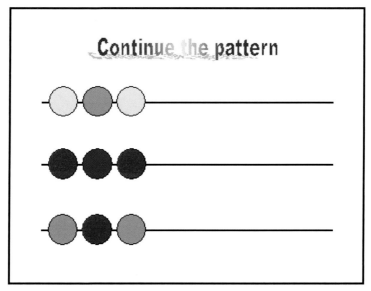

CD ROM: N28

Activity 29: Take away

Introduction

This activity introduces the children to subtraction. They also record, in the text box provided, the number of items left over after some have been taken away.

This resource could be readily amended by adding or deleting clip art to suit the needs of particular children.

Learning objectives

Early Learning Goals for Mathematical Development:

- Say and use number names in order in familiar contexts;
- Count reliably up to 10 everyday objects;
- Recognise numerals 1 to 9;
- Find one more or one less than a number from 1 to 10;
- Begin to relate addition to combining two groups of objects, and subtraction to 'taking away'.

National Numeracy Strategy Objectives:

Counting and recognising numbers
- Say and use number names in order in familiar contexts;

- Recite the number names in order, continuing the count forwards or backwards from a given number;
- Count reliably up to 10 everyday objects;
- Recognise numerals 1 to 9;

Adding and subtracting
- Find one more or one less than a number from 1 to 10;
- Begin to relate subtraction to 'taking away'.

More ideas!

- Explore 'take aways' using real objects;
- Explore 'take aways' up to 10;
- Draw the number of objects indicated;
- Record in numerals the number of objects shown.

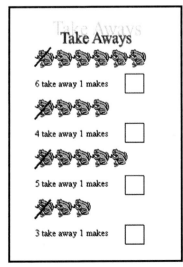

CD ROM: N29

Activity 30: Can you count?

Introduction

This simple counting activity enables individual children to enter the number of items shown within the text boxes provided.

This idea could be extended to simple addition and subtraction activities.

Learning objectives

Early Learning Goals for Mathematical Development:

- Say and use number names in order in familiar contexts;
- Count reliably up to 10 everyday objects;
- Recognise numerals 1 to 9.

National Numeracy Strategy Objectives:

Counting and recognising numbers
- Say and use number names in order in familiar contexts;
- Recite the number names in order, continuing the count forwards or backwards from a given number;
- Count reliably up to 10 everyday objects;
- Recognise numerals 1 to 9.

client ✓

More ideas!

- Explore counting using real objects;
- Explore counting up to 10 objects on screen;
- Draw / insert the number of objects indicated;
- Explore counting using a number line.

CD ROM: N30

Numeracy
Using PowerPoint

ICT & Numeracy and Mathematical Development - Using PowerPoint

Teacher ICT Skills Activity Checklist Activity:	CD ROM File	Load PowerPoint	Choose an Autolayout	Add a Background	Add AutoShapes	Add Clip Art	Animate Clip Art	Add Text Boxes	Animate text	Add a new slide	Run the presentation
Counting	N31	*	*	*		*	*	*	*		*
Counting on	N32	*	*	*		*	*	*	*		*
Find one more	N33	*	*	*		*	*	*	*	*	*
Counting in twos	N34	*	*	*		*	*	*	*		*
Counting in tens	N35	*	*	*				*	*	*	*
Combining groups	N36	*	*	*		*	*	*	*		*
Take away	N37	*	*	*		*	*	*	*	*	*
Name the shape	N38	*	*	*	*		*	*	*		*
Bigger and smaller	N39	*	*	*	*		*	*	*		*
Estimation	N40	*	*	*	*		*	*	*	*	*

Activity 31: Counting

Introduction

This presentation uses clip art with animation and sound to create a simple counting activity. You can use the presentation with the whole class counting aloud. This will help develop the children's ability to count reliably and also recognise numerals.

Additional slides and clip art will enable the resource to be extended to cover the numerals 1 to 10.

Learning objectives

Early Learning Goals for Mathematical Development:

- Say and use number names in order in familiar contexts;
- Count reliably up to 10 everyday objects;
- Recognise numerals 1 to 9.

client

National Numeracy Strategy Objectives:

Counting and recognising numbers
- Say and use number names in order in familiar contexts;
- Recite the number names in order, continuing the count forwards or backwards from a given number;
- Count reliably up to 10 everyday objects;
- Recognise numerals 1 to 9.

More ideas!

- Explore counting using concrete objects;
- Record the number of objects shown on screen;
- Draw a number of objects to match the numeral shown;
- Create a display with objects to count.

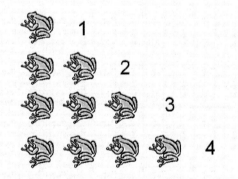

CD ROM: N31

Activity 32: Counting on

Introduction

This activity introduces children to the concept of addition by counting on. Two groups of objects are presented and the children are asked to find the total before clicking the mouse to reveal the answer.

The clip art used within this activity could easily be substituted for items relevant to the class topic.

Learning objectives

Early Learning Goals for Mathematical Development:

- Say and use number names in order in familiar contexts;
- Count reliably up to 10 everyday objects;
- Recognise numerals 1 to 9.

National Numeracy Strategy Objectives:

Counting and recognising numbers
- Say and use number names in order in familiar contexts;
- Recognise numerals 1 to 9;
- Begin to relate addition to counting on.

client ✓

More ideas!

- Explore 'counting on' using real objects;
- Explore 'counting on' using a number line presented on screen;
- Record the total number of objects shown on screen;
- Draw the number and total number of objects displayed in numerals.

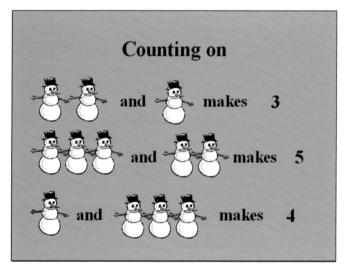

CD ROM: N32

Activity 33: Find one more

Introduction

Explore the concept of addition by asking children to 'Find one more' than a given number. At the click of the mouse a number of objects are presented on screen and then one more. The children find the total number of objects and then click to reveal the answer.

This idea could be extended to explore numbers from 1 to 10 and the clip art can be replaced with items appropriate to a variety of different topics.

Learning objectives

Early Learning Goals for Mathematical Development:

- Say and use number names in order in familiar contexts;
- Count reliably up to 10 everyday objects;
- Recognise numerals 1 to 9;
- Find one more or one less than a number from 1 to 10;
- Begin to relate addition to combining two groups of objects, and subtraction to 'taking away'.

client ✓

National Numeracy Strategy Objectives:

Counting and recognising numbers
- Say and use number names in order in familiar contexts;
- Recognise numerals 1 to 9;

Adding and subtracting
- Find one more or one less than a number from 1 to 10;
- Begin to relate addition to combining two groups of objects;
- Begin to relate addition to counting on.

More ideas!

- Explore 'Find one more' using real objects;
- Explore 'Find one more' using a number line presented on screen;
- Record the number of objects shown on screen;
- Draw the number and total number of objects displayed in numerals.

CD ROM: N33

Activity 34: Counting in twos

Introduction

This activity encourages the children to count in twos. Pairs of objects appear on the screen. In addition, the children's recognition of numerals is reinforced as these appear on the screen as they count.

Additional items could be added to explore numbers beyond 10 and / or adapted to explore counting in threes.

Learning objectives

Early Learning Goals for Mathematical Development:

- Say and use number names in order in familiar contexts;
- Count reliably up to 10 everyday objects;
- Recognise numerals 1 to 9.

National Numeracy Strategy Objectives:

Counting and recognising numbers
- Say and use number names in order in familiar contexts;
- Count in twos;
- Recognise numerals 1 to 9;

Adding and subtracting
- Begin to relate the addition of doubles to counting on.

More ideas!

- Explore 'counting in twos' using real objects;
- Explore 'counting in twos' using a number line presented on screen;
- Record the total number of objects shown on screen;
- Draw the number and total number of objects displayed in numerals.

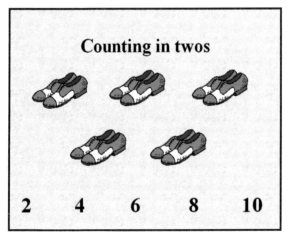

CD ROM: N34

Activity 35: Counting in tens

Introduction

This presentation reinforces children's number recognition whilst encouraging them to count in tens. Each multiple of 10 is presented at the click of a mouse in response to which children can count aloud as a whole class.

This resource could easily be adapted to help children to count from 1 to 10, or in twos, threes etc.

Learning objectives

Early Learning Goals for Mathematical Development:

- Say and use number names in order in familiar contexts.

National Numeracy Strategy Objectives:

Counting and recognising numbers
- Say and use number names in order in familiar contexts;
- Count in tens.

---

client ✓

More ideas!

- Explore 'counting in tens' with fingers;
- Explore 'counting in tens' using a number square;
- Record multiples of 10 on a number square.

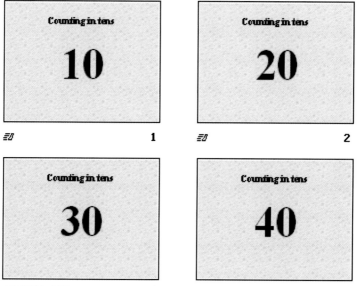

CD ROM: N35

Activity 36: Combining groups

Introduction

This activity will help the children explore the concept of addition by combining groups of objects. At the click of the mouse two groups of objects are presented and children identify the total of these two groups.

Similar resources could be created which explore any number bonds up to 10 and beyond.

Learning objectives

Early Learning Goals for Mathematical Development:

- Say and use number names in order in familiar contexts;
- Count reliably up to 10 everyday objects;
- Recognise numerals 1 to 9.

National Numeracy Strategy Objectives:

Counting and recognising numbers
- Say and use number names in order in familiar contexts;
- Recognise numerals 1 to 9;
- Adding and subtracting;
- Begin to relate addition to combining two groups of objects.

client ✓

More ideas!

- Explore 'Combining groups' using real objects;
- Complete 'Combining groups' activities on screen by *entering* the appropriate number;
- Complete 'Combining groups' activities on screen by *dragging* the correct number of objects into position;
- Complete 'Combining groups' activities by *drawing* the correct number of objects.

CD ROM: N36

Activity 37: Take away

Introduction

This activity introduces children to the concept of subtraction as 'taking away'. A small number of items are presented on screen and at the click of the mouse one item is taken away. Children are then asked to count how many are left.

This activity can be adapted by exploring 'take away' up to 10 and / or taking more than one item away at a time.

Learning objectives

Early Learning Goals for Mathematical Development:

- Say and use number names in order in familiar contexts;
- Count reliably up to 10 everyday objects;
- Recognise numerals 1 to 9;
- Find one more or one less than a number from 1 to 10;
- Begin to relate addition to combining two groups of objects, and subtraction to 'taking away'.

client ✓

National Numeracy Strategy Objectives:

Counting and recognising numbers
- Say and use number names in order in familiar contexts;
- Recognise numerals 1 to 9.

Adding and subtracting
- Find one more or one less than a number from 1 to 10;
- Begin to relate subtraction to 'taking away'.

More ideas!

- Explore 'taking away' using real objects;
- Complete 'take away' activities on screen by *entering* the appropriate number;
- Complete 'take away' activities on screen by *dragging* the correct number of objects into position;
- Complete 'take away' activities on paper by *drawing* the correct number of objects.

Take Aways

6 take away 1 makes ☐

4 take away 1 makes ☐

5 take away 1 makes ☐

3 take away 1 makes ☐

CD ROM: N37

Activity 38: Name the shape

Introduction

Within this activity, simple 2D shapes are presented at the click of a mouse. Children are then encouraged to identify each shape before clicking the mouse to reveal its name.

This presentation can be extended to include additional 2D and 3D shapes and / or be used as a stimulus for children's discussion of the properties of these shapes.

Learning objectives

Early Learning Goals for Mathematical Development:

- Use language such as 'circle' or 'bigger' to describe the shape and size of solids and flat shapes.

National Numeracy Strategy Objectives:

> **Measures, shape and space**
> - Use language such as circle or bigger to describe the shape and size of solids and flat shapes.

More ideas!

- Explore and name concrete 2D shapes;
- Label the shapes shown on screen;
- Drag the shape to its label on screen;
- Draw the appropriate shape next to its label;
- Create simple pictures using 2D shapes.

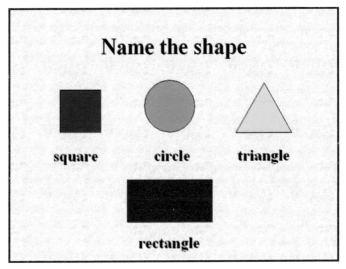

CD ROM: N38

Activity 39: Bigger and smaller

Introduction

This presentation reinforces children's shape recognition whilst introducing language related to measures, shape and space. The teacher encourages children to identify which of the two shapes presented is bigger or smaller before clicking the mouse to reveal the answer.

Similar resources can be created using a variety of autoshapes and / or clip art to encourage children to use language such as 'more' or 'less', 'longer' or 'shorter'.

Learning objectives

Early Learning Goals for Mathematical Development:

- Use language such as 'circle' or 'bigger' to describe the shape and size of solids and flat shapes.

National Numeracy Strategy Objectives:

> **Measures, shape and space**
> - Use language such as circle or bigger to describe the shape and size of solids and flat shapes.

More ideas!

- Explore 'bigger and smaller' using real objects;
- Draw big and small shapes;
- Label big and small shapes on screen;
- Explore language such as 'taller and shorter'.

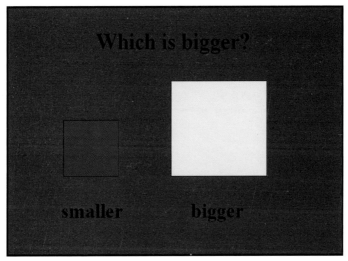

CD ROM: N39

Activity 40: Estimation

Introduction

This activity can be used to encourage children to estimate a number of objects and then check by counting. Click the mouse to reveal a number of counters before asking children to make their estimation. The actual number can be confirmed by counting and / or by clicking the mouse to reveal the answer.

You can adapt the presentation by replacing the counters with clip art appropriate to the class topic.

Learning objectives

Early Learning Goals for Mathematical Development:

- Say and use number names in order in familiar contexts;
- Count reliably up to 10 everyday objects;
- Recognise numerals 1 to 9.

National Numeracy Strategy Objectives:

Counting and recognising numbers
- Say and use number names in order in familiar contexts;
- Recite the number names in order, continuing the count forwards or backwards from a given number;

- Count reliably up to 10 everyday objects;
- Estimate a number in the range that can be counted reliably, then check by counting;
- Recognise numerals 1 to 9;

Solving problems

- Make simple estimates and predictions.

More ideas!

- Estimate the number within a collection of real objects;
- Record their estimate by writing a numeral;
- Estimate numbers within real contexts e.g. the number of cars in the car park;
- Explore estimation in other contexts such as length or weight.

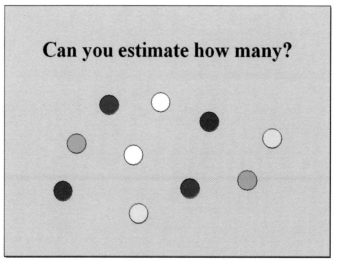

CD ROM: N40

More resources from

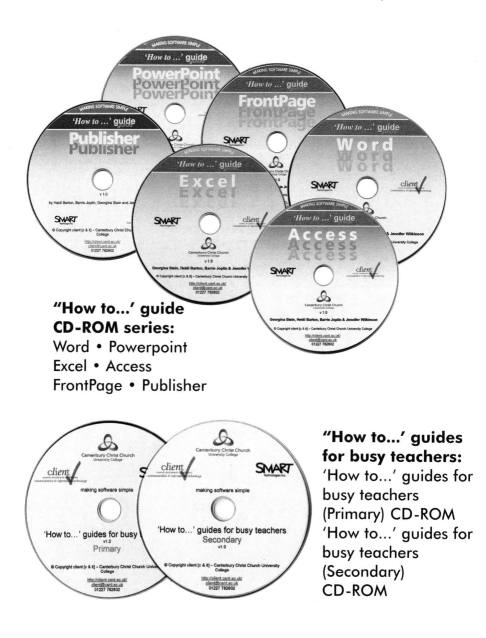

client
research, development & publication
communication & information technology

The client [c&it] unit has produced a wide range of publications and online resources for IT users and educators. For a regularly updated publications list go to: http://client.cant.ac.uk/publications/order.asp

"How to..." guide CD-ROM series:
Word • Powerpoint
Excel • Access
FrontPage • Publisher

"How to..." guides for busy teachers:
'How to...' guides for busy teachers (Primary) CD-ROM
'How to...' guides for busy teachers (Secondary) CD-ROM

'How to ...' flip-guides